BY GREEN FIG

Prophets' Stories

History of the Most Noble Mission

Volume 1

Design & Art by

Guzel Murtazina

NOTE:

Pictures in this book

don't correspond to reality

Publisher: Green Fig

Pennsylvania, USA

gogreenfig.com

ISBN 978-1953836588 (pbc)

CONTENTS

INTRODUCTION	7
WHO ARE THE PROPHETS?	9
How Many Prophets Were There?	12
Virtues of the Prophets	12
PROPHET ADAM ﷺ	14
The Creation of Adam ﷺ	14
The Day In Which Adam ﷺ Was Created	16
The Angels Greets Adam, but Satan Refuses	17
Eve—the First Woman	18
Life of Adam and Eve in Paradise	18
The Life of Adam and Eve on Earth	19
Adam—the First Prophet and Messenger	21
Kaabah—the First Mosque on Earth	21
Al-Aqsa Mosque	22
Children of Adam and Eve	23
Qabeel and Habeel	23
Death of Adam and Eve	26

The Honor of Prophet Adam ﷺ	27
PROPHET SHEETH ﷺ	28
PROPHET IDREES ﷺ	29
Call of Prophet Idrees ﷺ	29
Sciences of Prophet Idrees ﷺ	30
Emigration of Prophet Idrees to Egypt	31
How did Blasphemy Appear on Earth?	32
PROPHET NŪH ﷺ	34
Prophet Nūh's Ark ﷺ	35
The Big Flood	36
Humanity after the Global Flood	38
PROPHET HŪD ﷺ	39
The People of Prophet Hūd ﷺ	40
Punishment and death of the people of 'Ād	41
The People of Thamud	44
PROPHET SALIH ﷺ	44
The camel of Prophet Salih ﷺ	45
Punishment of the Thamudians	47

PROPHET AL-KHADIR 48

The story of Al-Khadir ﷺ 48

PROPHET IBRAHIM ﷺ 50

The Birth of Ibrahim ﷺ 50

Prophethood of Ibrahim ﷺ 51

Ibrahim ﷺ Destroys the Idols 52

The Debate between Prophet Ibrahim ﷺ and the Tyrant King 53

The Miracle of the Resurrection of the Birds 54

The Big Fire and the Big Miracle 55

Emigration of Prophet Ibrahim ﷺ to Sham 56

The Demise of Numrud 57

The call of the people of Harran 57

Travel to Egypt 58

Birth of Isma'il 59

The appearance of Zamzam Water 60

Arrival of the Jurhum tribe to Mecca 62

The story of Prophet Ibrahim's Sacrifice ﷺ 63

Construction of the Holy Kaabah 65

The News of Ishaq	67
The High Status of Prophet Ibrahim ﷺ	68
PROPHET ISMA'IL ﷺ	**69**
PROPHET ISHAQ ﷺ	**70**
PROPHET LUT ﷺ	**71**
People of Prophet Lut ﷺ	71
Guests of the Prophet Lut ﷺ	72
Punishment of the inhabitants of Sodom	74
PROPHET SHU'AYB ﷺ	**75**
The Origin of the Prophet Shu'ayb ﷺ	75
The call of Prophet Shu'ayb ﷺ to Monotheism	75
Punishment of Madyan people	76
EPILOGUE	**78**

INTRODUCTION

Dear young readers, As-salamu 'alaykum!

If you are reading these lines now, it's time to embark on an exciting journey! This book recounts the lives of the best people on earth and the stories that happened to them. As you read, you'll not only discover fascinating details about the lives of the prophets but also find answers to questions, and perhaps, see the world that surrounds you in a whole new light.

The belief in the prophets is an integral part of Faith (Imān), as taught to us by our beloved Prophet Muhammad (مُحَمَّد) ﷺ.

Imān is:

1. Believing in Allāh without associating partners with Him.

2. Believing in the angels, who never commit any sin and always obey Allāh's commands.

3. Believing in the Holy Books.

4. Believing in the prophets sent to guide us and teach the truth.

5. Believing in the Day of Judgment, when humans and jinns will be judged.

6. Believing in Al-Qadar, which means that everything in this universe happens by the Will of Allāh.

Allāh is not a man, angel, or like anything else we can imagine. However, we can contemplate the traces of His Power. Look around, and you will see many amazing creatures, all created by Allāh the Almightly! He created the heavens, the earth, and all of us. Additionally, Paradise and Hell were created by Him. Paradise is a place where believers will be rewarded for their faith and good deeds, while Hell is prepared for those who deserve punishment due to their bad deeds.

Allāh has established rules and laws for us, known as "Shari'ah." By following these rules, we find true happiness. We all desire to reach Paradise and enjoy eternal happiness in the Hereafter. To achieve this, we must follow the path of the prophets.

Take the time to read each chapter carefully and remember these amazing stories.

We wish you a pleasant journey!

WHO ARE THE PROPHETS?

The Belief in the prophets is one of the foundations of Islam. Prophets are the best of all the creations. Allāh the Almighty sent them to people to call for the Religion of Islam. All the prophets taught people that this world has a creator—Allāh, and that only Allāh deserves to be worshipped. All the Prophets, without exception, were believers in the One God, and none of them associated partners with Him. All the Prophets were Muslims; they ordered people to do good deeds and forbade doing evil.

Among the prophets were the messengers to whom Allāh revealed a new set of laws (Shari'ah); some of these laws differed from the ones revealed to the messenger before him. These laws determined what was permissible and what was forbidden and taught people how to live and do acts of worship correctly. They taught ablution, prayers, judgments about marriage and many other things.

All prophets, whether messengers or not, called people to Islam, received the revelation, and conveyed to others what they were ordered to convey.

To some prophets, Allāh gave the Holy Books or Scriptures. These sacred books were sent down in different languages. There were 104 Books in total. The last of them is the Holy Qur'an revealed to our Prophet Muhammad ﷺ. The Qur'an will be preserved until the end of the world, while the previous books have been either distorted or not present anymore with people.

Family Tree of the 25 Prophets mentioned in the Qur'an

10

Family Tree of the 25 Prophets mentioned in the Qur'an

Adam — **Sheeth (Sheth)** — Anūsh — Qeynān — Mihlaīl — Yard — **Idrīs (Enoch)** — Mattūshalah — Lāmak — **Nūḥ (Noah)**

From Nūḥ's line (Sām — Arabs, Persians, Romans): Arfahshadh — Irum — Qynān — Shaliḥ — Ghābir — Fāleygh — Arghū — Sārugh — Nāhir — Āzar (Tārih) — **Ibrāhīm (Abraham)**

From Nūḥ's other sons:
- Yāfith — Turks, Slavs, Gog and Magog (with 'Awj, Al-Jaūd, Rāsūkh, Qaḥṭān, Mahan, 'Abdallāh — **Hūd**, **Al-Khaḍir**)
- Hām — Copts, Berbers, Africans (with 'Ubayd, Mīsāh, Thamūd, Hāḍir, 'Āthir — **Ṣāliḥ**)

From **Ibrāhīm (Abraham)**:
- Ḥarān — **Lūṭ (Lot)** — Lut's daughter — **Shu'ayb** — Yā'rub, Nābit
- **Ismā'īl (Ishmael)**
- **Isḥāq (Isaac)** — **Ya'qūb (Jacob)** — Al-'Īṣ, Shamā'ūn, Yashkur, Iṣāḥār, Rafqat, Yaʿqūb's daughter, Batuīl, Nāgur — **Yūsuf (Joseph)** — Afrāyīm — Shūtalḥ — **Yūshā'**

11

How Many Prophets Were There?

Throughout the history of humankind, there have been many prophets—about 124,000! Of these, 313 of those were messengers. We only know the names of some of them. The Holy Qur'an mentions the names of 25 prophets. The first prophet and messenger was Adam ﷺ, and the last was Muhammad ﷺ, the best of all the prophets!

The prophets were people from different nations and spoke different languages, but they all called for One God and their religion was Islam.

Virtues of the Prophets

Allāh entrusted the prophets with a special mission—to call people to the true religion and bring Shari'ah to them. This is a great and honorable work, and it is entrusted to the most worthy! Therefore, the prophets are the best creations of Allāh and the most honorable of people. Allāh the Almighty gave His chosen ones the most beautiful attributes. All prophets, without exception, were intelligent, sincere, honest, courageous, kind, generous, truthful and eloquent. They were never cowards, they never betrayed, and they never committed even the slightest meanness. All the Prophets were beautiful, with great manners because these attributes make them more attractive to people and more likely to be accepted by them. Allāh gave all the prophets great miracles. A miracle is an extraordinary matter that proves the truthfulness of the prophet and cannot be challenged.

Prophets have always been believers (Muslims) even if they lived among unbelievers. They never worshiped anyone but Allāh, and did not commit acts of blasphemy—neither before receiving the revelation of the prophethood, nor after. The Creator endowed his chosen ones with wisdom and patience. Allāh also gave them great trials to show us the greatness of their character and their high status. Their life is an example for us and a support in life's difficult situations.

PROPHET ADAM ﷺ

Adam ﷺ is the father of all the humans. We are used to seeing every person has parents—mother and father. Usually people are born small and helpless, and then they grow up, get married, and have children. Many generations of people replace each other. Now there are billions of people on earth! And in the entire history of humanity lived even more! How did humans appear on Earth? Where did they come from?

Adam is the first human created by Allāh. He was created in Paradise, lived there for 130 years, and then descended to the earth. He is the forefather of all people, that is, he is their common ancestor. Every human who has ever lived is a descendant of Adam. Adam was not only the first man, but also the first Prophet—he believed in the One Creator and called on other people to worship God.

The Creation of Adam ﷺ

Of all the kind of creations, the humankind was created last. Before humans, Allāh created angels and jinn (genies). Angels were created from light, while jinn were created from fire. Adam was the first man and he was created from the soil of the earth. Allāh ordered an angel to take from the earth we live on a handful of different types of soil and bring the collected soil to Paradise. There, this soil was mixed with water from underneath the throne, and from this clay the shape of Adam was created. After the clay dried, God turned it into flesh, bones, and blood. Then the soul entered this body, and Adam became alive. The first words he spoke were "Alhamdulillāh", which means "Praise be to Allāh!" From the very beginning, Adam knew that Allāh is the Creator of everything, and that only Allāh is worthy of worship.

The name "Adam" comes from the Arabic word "adeem", which means "top layer of the earth" or "soil". The descendants of Adam are different in skin color and character because of the different types of soil from which Adam was created. There are people with white skin, red, black, and in between. Among them there are the soft and the harsh, and in between. There are also the bad ones and the good ones, and in between. Prophet Muhammad ﷺ said:

"Allāh the Almighty sent an angel who took from this earth's soil a handful of white, black and that which is between, as well as bad, good and that which is between. And that is why the descendants of Adam are so different."

The Day In Which Adam ﷺ Was Created

The first creation of Allāh was water. God created all the other creations from water. The second creation was the Throne, followed by the Higher Pen then the Guarded Tablet. Allāh created the heavens and earths in six days that began on a Sunday, fifty-thousand years after the Pen wrote on the Guarded Tablet everything that will happen until Judgment Day. Adam was created in Paradise at the last hour of Friday, the last of those 6 days. Those days were not like our usual days. Each day of these six were equal to fifty-thousand of the days we know. Prophet Muhammad ﷺ said:

"The best day of the week is Friday, on this day Adam was created."

Allāh endowed Adam with a beautiful appearance and voice. He had an excellent shape and a beautiful face. He was much taller than the humans were nowadays. The height of Adam was 60 cubits, which is more than 25 meters. This is about as tall as an 8-story building! At the shoulders, he was seven cubits wide. Adam was erect and walked on two feet. Prophet Muhammad described him in the hadeeth to be tall like a palm tree.

The Angels Greets Adam, but Satan Refuses

Allāh has given the humans special endowments over His other creations. He created the first man in a beautiful image, endowed him with a soul and a mind, and gave him the true faith. When the soul entered the body of Adam, he came to life. Allāh the Almighty ordered the angels to greet the first human by prostrating to him. The angels fulfilled this order, since they are all always obedient to Allāh.

At that time, the forefather of all jinn (genies) lived in Paradises with the angels. His name was 'Azazeel. He, too, was ordered to prostrate to Adam to greet him, but he refused. Out of pride and envy, he said, "I am better than Adam. You created me from fire, and him from clay", believing that fire is better than clay. Due to his arrogance, he refused to fulfill the order of Allāh and objected to Him. By this action 'Azazeel blasphemed, this means he became a non-believer. He was no more a Muslim. After that, he was cursed and named "Iblees", which in Arabic means "devoid of the mercy of Allāh".

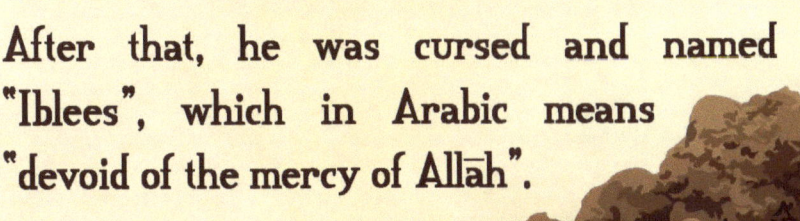

Eve-the First Woman

Adam lived alone in Paradise for some time before Allāh created a woman to be Adam's wife. Hawwa' (Eve) was the first woman. Her name comes from the Arabic word "ḥayy", which means "alive". She was named like that because Allāh created her from the rib of Adam, that is, from a living being. Eve was beautiful. She loved Adam and Adam loved her. Adam and Eve were Muslims. Adam ﷺ and his wife Eve were the first married couple. Like Adam, Eve was created as an adult. She was tall to match Prophet Adam's size. All humans after them 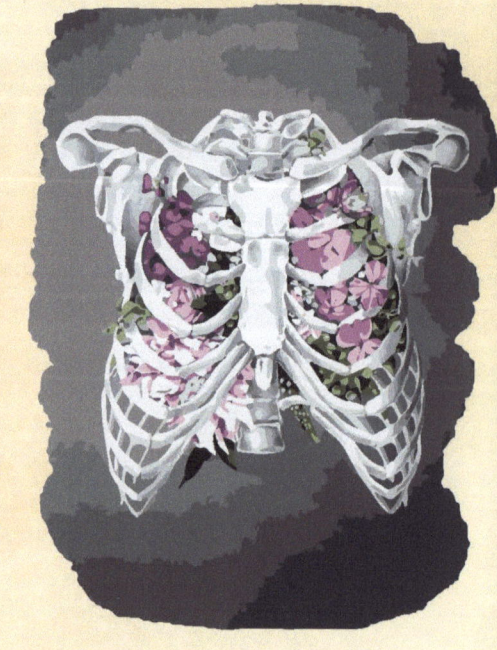 are born small and gradually grow up. Adam and Eve, by the Will of Allāh, were created as adults from the beginning and had no parents. Indeed, Allāh has power over everything!

Life of Adam and Eve in Paradise

The life of Adam and Eve in Paradise was happy and comfortable. They lived among beautiful nature, did not get sick, did not get tired and did not get upset. They wore clothes of light, and they always had delicious food and drink. Allāh allowed them to enjoy all the blessings of Paradise, except for a single tree, the fruits of which they were forbidden to eat. Nevertheless, one day they ate from the fruits of this tree, thereby committing a small sin. This means they did something they were prohibited from doing by the order of Allāh, their Creator. However, Adam and Eve soon regretted what they did and repented from this sin. Allāh accepted their repentance and forgave them. Prophets are the best and the most honorable creations of Allāh. They never commit blasphemy, big sins, and small sins that are demeaning. Moreover, if any prophet make a small sin that is not demeaning, he immediately repents and asks Allāh for forgiveness. A demeaning small sin is one that indicates lowness of character; this is impossible to be done by a prophet. Prophets have the highest character. Adam's eating from this tree was a small sin but not a demeaning one.

The Life of Adam and Eve on Earth

After eating the forbidden fruit, Adam and Eve realized their mistake, repented of their sin, and Allāh forgave them, but they were destined to leave Paradise and come down to live on Earth.

Adam received the revelation of prophethood on earth. In total, Adam lived for 1000 years; 130 years in Paradise and the rest of the time on earth. The day Adam left Paradise and descended to earth was a Friday. Adam and  Eve landed on earth in different places: Adam—on the island of Sarandeeb (Sri Lanka) not far from the coast of India, and Eve—in Jeddah area in the Arabian Peninsula. They were reunited in a plain called "Muzdalifah" between Mecca and 'Arafat. As for Iblees, the damned, he was expelled from Paradise in disgrace and cast down to earth. Allāh let Adam know that Iblees is an enemy for him and for all humanity.

In Paradise, Adam was given the knowledge of the names of all things. For example, he knew the words "earth", "water", "trees", etc. in all languages. Prophet Adam knew all languages and was eloquent—he spoke clearly and beautifully. On earth, the life of Adam and Eve was not as easy as in Paradise. In Paradise, they did not have to make any effort to have food, drink and clothing, but on Earth, they had to work a lot. Allāh gave Adam all the necessary knowledge for life on Earth: how to make tools such as shovels and sickles,

how to plow the land, sow grain, harvest crops, make flour and bake bread from it, as well as how to grow vegetables and fruits. He knew how to sew clothes and build houses. Adam knew how to mint gold and silver coins too.

Adam-the First Prophet and Messenger

On Earth, Adam received the revelation from Allāh and became a Prophet. He was given the Sharī'ah, the laws that the people had to follow. Adam taught his family how to worship Allāh and to perform the rituals of Islam like ablution and prayer. Adam also taught his children to be honest, kind, and sincere. Like all prophets, Adam was a Muslim, and all of his descendants at his time were Muslims too.

Kaabah-the First Mosque on Earth

Allah ordered Prophet Adam ﷺ to build the Sacred House—the Kaabah on the land of the future city of Mecca. To build the Kaabah, Adam used the stones of five mountains that were located on different lands: Mount Sinai in Egypt, Mount Zaita in Palestine, Mount Lebanon in Lebanon, Mount Judy in Iraq, and Mount Hira', which is located in the vicinity of Mecca where Prophet Muhammad ﷺ received the first revelation.

These stones were laid as the foundation of the Kaabah. When the construction of the Kaabah was completed, Allāh ordered Angel Jibreel (Gabriel) to teach Adam the rituals of the Hajj (Pilgrimage). The Kaabah remained unchanged in the form in which it was built by Prophet Adam ﷺ, until the Flood, which occurred during the time of Prophet Nūh ﷺ. During the Flood, the buildings were destroyed. Later, Prophet Ibrahim ﷺ rebuilt the Kaabah in its original place. The Kaabah is the very first mosque and most honorable building on earth. The place where the Kaabah is located is the center of the inhabited earth. Above the earthly Kaabah in the Seventh Heaven is Bayt al-Ma'mour, which is the Kaabah for the angels in the skies.

Al-Aqsa Mosque

Forty years after the construction of the Kaabah, Prophet Adam ﷺ built the Farthest Mosque (Al-Aqsa) in Palestine on the territory of the future city of Al-Quds (Jerusalem). Al-Aqsa Mosque is a very important place for Muslims. It was to this mosque that Prophet Muhammad ﷺ went during his miraculous night journey of Al-Isra' from Mecca to Jerusalem, which he made accompanied by the head angel Jibreel, on the back of a riding animal from Paradise. In this mosque, Prophet Muhammad ﷺ was given an

amazing thing—all the prophets were gathered and they all prayed together, and Prophet Muhammad ﷺ was their imam! It is from Al-Aqsa, that Prophet Muhammad ascended to the seven heavens, where he saw the amazing wonders of the upper world.

Children of Adam and Eve

In Paradise, Adam and Eve had no children. Their children were all born on Earth. Lady Eve was pregnant 40 times—every time she delivered a twin of a boy and a girl except once, only one boy was born—this was the future Prophet Sheth ﷺ. Since there were no other people on earth at that time, the children of Adam and Eve married each other for the humans race to continue. Therefore, according to the Shari'ah of Adam, a brother could marry his sister if she was not his twin. It was forbidden for one to marry his twin sister.

Qabeel and Habeel

Qabeel (Cain) and Habeel (Abel) were brothers—the sons of Prophet Adam ﷺ. Habeel was a kind, God-fearing, generous and good person, while Kabeel was evil, cruel, envious and greedy. When they grew up, they wanted to marry the same girl. Prophet Adam ordered each of them to make a sacrifice (qurban) to see who would be the one to marry

her. Habeel had a flock of sheep and Qabeel had a field of wheat. Habeel was God-fearing and took the best ram for his qurban—big and fat. Qabeel, took a sheaf of wheat of the worst varieties for his qurban.

Allāh accepted the sacrifice of Habeel while the qurban of Qabeel was not accepted and remained untouched. The sign that the qurban was accepted was that a fire would descend from the sky and take away this qurban. Seeing that his brother's qurban was accepted but not his, Qabeel became very angry. He began to threaten his brother to kill him so that he would not marry that girl.

Habeel said to him: "Allāh accepts sacrifice from the God-fearing." Qabeel had hatred for his brother in his heart.

Once, when Habeel stayed late in the pasture with his flock and did not return at the usual time, Prophet Adam became worried and sent Qabeel to find out if something had happened to his brother. Qabeel went to him and when he met Habeel, he said to him, "Allāh accepted your qurban, but mine was not accepted!" Habeel answered him in the same way as before, "Verily, Allāh accepts the qurban from the pious." Qabeel again became furious and began to threaten his brother to kill him.

Habeel said: "Even if you raise your hand to kill me, I will not raise my hand to kill you. Indeed, I fear the punishment of Allāh—

the Lord of all the worlds! If you kill me, you will have responsibility for that sin and deserve punishment in hell. This is what awaits sinners!"

Qabeel was much weaker than Habeel, so he decided to wait until his brother fell asleep in order to kill him. When Habeel went to sleep, Qabeel approached him and hit him on the head with a heavy stone, Qabeel killed his brother! In the north of Damascus, on Mount Qasiyun, there is a cave, which is called the "cave of blood." It is said that this is the place where Qabeel killed his brother Habeel. After killing his brother, Qabeel did not know what to do with his body. He did not want to carry him to his father, so that he would not be sad. Not knowing what to do, Qabeel carried Habeel's body until it began to smell.

Birds of prey circled above him, and beasts followed him, waiting for him to drop the body to eat it. Kabeel regretted that he had killed his brother, but this was not a repentance for his big sin; rather he only regretted that he did not know what to do with the dead body. At this time, two crows flew in and began to fight. One crow killed another and began to dig he ground with its beak. Having dug a hole, he threw the dead crow into it and covered it with earth.

Then Qabeel exclaimed, "What a fool I am! I didn't even think to do what the crow did, and I couldn't hide my brother's body!" Following the example of the crow, Qabeel buried the body of Habeel in the ground.

Killing without a right is a great sin, and Qabeel was the first to commit this sin. The cause of this terrible crime was his envy of his brother, just as envy of Adam became the cause of blasphemy of Iblees. However, Qabeel remained a Muslim and did not object to Allāh like Iblees.

Prophet Muhammad ﷺ said:

"Every time someone kills a Muslim unjustly, the son of Adam, Qabeel, also receives a sin for this, because he is the first to commit this murder."

Death of Adam and Eve

Prophet Adam ﷺ lived 1000 years: 130 years in Paradise, and the rest of the time on earth. According to some sayings, he was buried in the area of Mina near Mecca. Hundreds of years later, when the Flood began, Prophet Nūh ﷺ took the body of Prophet Adam ﷺ into the ark. After the Flood, the descendants of Nūh buried him in a place that Prophet

Adam himself indicated in his will. It was narrated that after the death of Adam, Eve lived only one year and was buried in the area of Jeddah.

During all the life Prophet Adam ﷺ and for another 1000 years after his death, all humanity followed the religion of Islam. Blasphemy only appeared after the death of Prophet Idrees ﷺ the third prophet.

The Honor of Prophet Adam ﷺ

Many people do not know where humanity came from. Some people mistakenly believe that humans evolved from monkeys—they claim that monkeys, gradually changing and developing, eventually turned into people. Therefore, some people think that Adam looked like a monkey, walked without clothes and could not talk, but communicated with sounds and gestures. This is contrary to the teachings of Islam and humiliates the dignity of Prophet Adam ﷺ. The first humans—Adam and Eve—were not like animals! They did not move on all four members; they walked on two legs. They communicated in a clear, beautiful language. They were not naked, but wore clothes—both in Paradise and on earth. From the very beginning of life on earth, humanity had a civilization and was not a primitive society of savages. People had knowledge, morality and law, and they owed this to our forefather—Prophet Adam ﷺ. It was Adam who taught people the words: "There is no God but Allāh!"

PROPHET SHEETH ﷺ

Prophet Sheeth ﷺ (Sheth) was the son of Adam ﷺ and a prophet and messenger. Prophet Adam named him "Sheeth" which means "God's gift". From birth, Sheeth was special—he was the only son of Adam who was born without a twin sister. Sheeth was born after the death of Habeel.

After the death of Adam, Allāh the Almighty gave Sheeth the Revelation of prophethood ﷺ. At that time, all people were Muslims, and Sheeth continued the mission of his father urging the people to be God-fearing. Sheeth was given a new sharia (shari'ah). According to this sharia, a brother could not marry his own sister, since by that time there were already many more people on earth. Allāh gave Sheeth 50 Holy books called Sahaif.

Prophet Sheeth lived in Mecca and died at the age of 912 years. After the death of Prophet Sheeth ﷺ, people continued to be on the religion of Islam and lived according to its Sharia until the third Prophet appeared— Idrees ﷺ.

PROPHET IDREES ﷺ

The third Messenger of Allāh after Adam ﷺ and Sheeth ﷺ was Idrees ﷺ. He is also named Akhnoukh (Enoch), though he is more known by the name Idrees, which comes from the Arabic word dirasah, which means "study".

Since his childhood, he spent lot of time studying the knowledge passed along from prophets Adam ﷺ and Sheeth ﷺ. Idrees was Sheeth's great-great-grandson; this means there were four generations between them. By that time, the descendants of Adam had settled over large areas. Idrees was born in the city of Babylon in today's Iraq.

Call of Prophet Idrees ﷺ

During the time of Idrees ﷺ too, Islam was the only religion on earth. Idrees received the revelation and a new Sharia. Prophet Idrees was given 30 Holy Books called sahaif. At his time, people spoke 72 languages. Allāh the Almighty gave Prophet Idrees ﷺ the knowledge of all these languages, and he addressed every nation in its language. Prophet Idrees ﷺ called on people to be God-fearing—to do what Allāh commanded and not to do what Allāh forbade. He tirelessly reminded people that they will be rewarded in Paradise for their good deeds, and will be punished for the bad deeds. He encouraged people to be careful in performing the rituals of the Religion like prayers, ablution, and fasting. Prophet Idrees

ﷺ told the people that the intoxicating drinks are forbidden. He urged people to be modest, be content with little in this temporary life and treat each other fairly. Prophet Idrees ﷺ became famous for his eloquence and strong sermons, as well as his wise sayings. One of the sayings of Prophet Idrees ﷺ is: "Patience with faith will lead to victory." It is narrated that these words were carved on a precious stone on his ring.

Sciences of Prophet Idrees ﷺ

Like Prophet Adam ﷺ, Prophet Idrees ﷺ knew how to cut and sew clothes. He had a job as a tailor. He also knew how to write. He was the first to write using a pen, which in those days was a special stick with a pointed end. Allāh gave Prophet Idrees ﷺ special knowledges which he passed on to people. He gave him the knowledge of the science of astronomy which is the science of the outer space and the bodies in it like the stars, the planets and

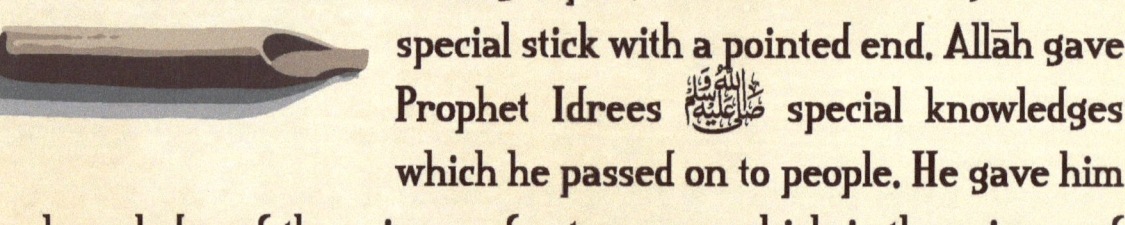

their location. He was also given the knowledge of how to make a calendar. Prophet Idrees ﷺ established many holidays for his people on certain dates. Prophet Idrees ﷺ had a deep knowledge of medicine. He was also the first who taught people the science of the construction of cities according to a plan. At his time, each nation built cities on its land based on this knowledge. During his lifetime, 88 cities were built.

Emigration of Prophet Idrees to Egypt

Prophet Idrees ﷺ urged Muslims to observe the rules of the Religion. However, not everyone listened to him. Some refused to obey him and continued to sin. Therefore, Prophet Idrees ﷺ decided to move from Babylon to another area. His followers moved with him. It was not easy for them to leave their hometowns so they said to Prophet Idrees ﷺ, "Where can we find a place like our Babylon if we leave it ?!" The word "Babylon" in Aramaic language means "river". They meant the Tigris and Euphrates rivers because they lived in their valley. Prophet Idrees ﷺ answered them, "If we make this emigration sincerely for the sake of Allāh, then Allāh will grant us another blessed place." So Prophet Idrees ﷺ, together with his followers, left Iraq. They reached Egypt, where they saw the majestic Nile River. They liked the new place. Prophet Idrees ﷺ stopped at the Nile and began to praise the Creator, saying: "SubhanAllāh!", That is, "Allāh is clear of any imperfection!" Then, Prophet Idrees ﷺ lived with his followers in Egypt, calling people to obey the Creator.

Prophet Idrees ﷺ, like all the prophets, was very patient and accomplished his mission. Idrees was granted a special miracle—he ascended to Heaven! After some time, Prophet Idrees ﷺ was returned to the Earth where he died.

How did Blasphemy Appear on Earth?

Prophet Idrees ﷺ lived at the end of the first millennium (one thousand years) after the death of Prophet Adam ﷺ. At the time of Prophets Adam, Sheeth and Idrees, all people were Muslims, that is, they believed in the One and Only Creator and worshiped only Him. But sometime after the death of Prophet Idrees ﷺ, Iblees the devil came to the people in the form of a man. He had an evil plan to lead humanity astray. He ordered people to make statues of five saints—students of Prophet Idrees ﷺ, who were no longer alive. He told them that these statues would keep them from forgetting these good teachers. People listened and made these five statues. As time went on, people's knowledge became less and less, and they sinned more and more. Many years after he first appeared, Iblees came to the people again and this time ordered them to worship these statues, saying that these were their "gods". Some people listened to him and began to worship these statues, making them their idols. These people became blasphemers.

PROPHET NŪH ﷺ

Prophet Nūh ﷺ came one thousand years after the death of Prophet Idrees ﷺ. During this time, falsehood and blasphemy spread more and more among people until not a single believer remained on earth. This period is called "the first era of ignorance (jahiliyyah)". Then, Allāh sent Nūh ﷺ to be a prophet to the people. Nūh was the great-grandson of Prophet Idrees ﷺ. Nūh was the first prophet who was sent to unbelievers to call them to Islam. Nūh ﷺ told his people to stop worshiping statues that do not create anything, and to believe in the One and Only Creator—Allāh.

He said, "Oh my people! Worship only Allāh—There is no creator other than Him! Believe and be God-fearing!"

Prophet Nūh ﷺ also warned of the terrible punishment that awaits them if they do not stop worshiping idols and accept Islam. Nūh called his people to the Faith for a very long time—950 years, but only few followed him.

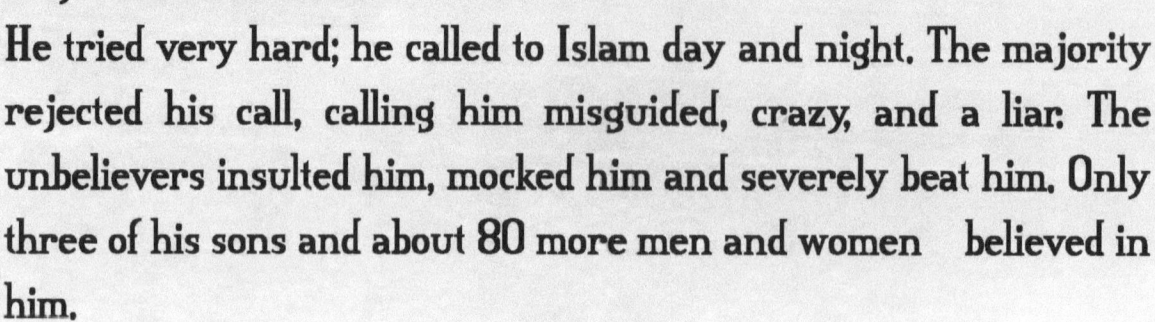

He tried very hard; he called to Islam day and night. The majority rejected his call, calling him misguided, crazy, and a liar. The unbelievers insulted him, mocked him and severely beat him. Only three of his sons and about 80 more men and women believed in him.

Prophet Nuh's Ark ﷺ

For many years, Prophet Nūh ﷺ called his people to Islam. Despite all his efforts, their evil and sins only increased, and each new generation was even worse than the previous one. People said: "He was the same 'crazy' back in the days of our fathers and grandfathers, and we will not listen to him either."

After 950 years of calling them to Islam, Prophet Nūh ﷺ received from Allah the revelation that no one would believe in him anymore. Then, Nūh ﷺ made a supplication and said:

"O my Lord! Let not a single unbeliever remain on earth! For if You preserve their lives, they will lead people astray and will not give birth to anyone but unbelieving sinners."

Prophet Nūh ﷺ then knew that the unbelievers would be destroyed. Allah ordered him to build an ark—a large ship that would save Muslims during the upcoming terrible disaster.

Allah granted Prophet Nūh ﷺ the knowledge of how to make an ark. Nūh ﷺ collected everything that was needed: wooden boards, iron, tar and other materials, and started building the ship.

The unbelievers, passing near Nūh, laughed at the fact that he was building a ship in the desert, because there was no sea nearby. Mocking him, they said, "O Nūh! Have you become a carpenter after being a Prophet?!"

Nūh built the ark out of teak wood from a tree that sprouted the day he was born. Over the lifetime of Nūh, it has grown and became huge. The ark was 80 cubits long, 50 cubits wide, and 30 cubits high. It consisted of three tiers: the lower one for animals, the middle one for people and the upper one for birds. The Ark of Nūh was the first ship in the history of humankind—no one had built anything similar before!

The Big Flood

The hour of punishment for blasphemy and sins came! Water began to come out from inside the earth to its surface. This went on for 40 days! After the earth released all its water, rain poured from the sky like continuous streams in a way that had never happened before—each drop was like a mountain! If this rain had come before the underground water came to the surface, these huge drops would have destroyed the mountains, and the earth would have been covered with cracks! A heavy downpour went on for another 40 days without stopping. There was so much water that it covered the whole earth—even the highest mountains! There has never been such a disaster before! When the flood began, the animals, fleeing from the water, ran to the ark. Prophet Nūh ﷺ took on the ship a pair from all kinds of animals and birds—a male and a female. Nūh, three of his sons with their wives and the rest of the believers – about 83 of them, entered the ark. It was the 10th day of the month of Rajab. Prophet Nūh's ark floated among the waves that were as tall as mountains, but by the Will of Allāh, all its inhabitants remained safe. As for the unbelievers, they all perished. Among them was the fourth son of Nūh, Kanʿan, who refused to embrace Islam. After 40 days of continuous rain, Allāh ordered the sky to stop the rain and the earth to absorb the water. All the water seeped inside the earth and its surface returned to how it was before the flood.

The amazing voyage of the believers in the ark of Prophet Nūh ﷺ lasted 150 days! During this voyage, the ark sailed over the area of ʿArafat, then it sailed to the territory of Muzdalifah, then to Mina, where pilgrims during the Hajj throw stones. Then the ark sailed to the Kaabah and made seven circles around it, and then sailed seven times between the hills of As-Safa and Al-Marwah. There are the places where pilgrims go during

Hajj. The ark sailed on and after a while, it ended up over Mount Judy in nowadays Iraq and landed there. After a month, the earth dried up and it was possible to go out. This makes the total duration Nuh and his followers stayed inside the ark six months! The day they landed on mount Judy was the day of 'Ashoora', the 10th of the month of Al-Muharram. On this day, Prophet Nuh ﷺ fasted, thanking Allah for their salvation!

Humanity after the Global Flood

After the Flood, not a single unbeliever remained. The earth was settled by the descendants of the sons of Prophet Nuh ﷺ—Sam, Ham and Yafith. As for the other believers, they had no children after they came out from the ark. The three sons of Nuh had children, then grandchildren, then great-grandchildren and so on until there were many people again.

Prophet Nuh ﷺ lived a very long life—1780 years! He received the Revelation at the age of 480. Before the Flood, he called people to Islam for 950 years, and after the flood, he lived for another 350 years. Nuh is among the five best prophets who are in order of their merit: Muhammad, Abraham, Moses, Jesus and Nuh.

PROPHET HŪD ﷺ

After Allah saved Prophet Nūh and the other believers from the Flood, and all the unbelievers were destroyed, the descendants of his three sons settled the earth: Sam, Ham and Yafith. As time went by, people settled on more and more territories, some began to move away from the Faith. The first ones to worship the idols after the Great Flood were the people of 'Ād. Allāh the Almighty sent Prophet Hūd to them who was a descendant of Sam, one of Prophet Nūh's son. Hūd ﷺ was an Arab.

Prophet Muhammad said, ﷺ:

"There were four Arabs among the prophets: Hūd, Sālih, Shu'ayb and your prophet, meaning himself– Muhammad."

Prophet Hūd ﷺ belonged to the people of 'Ād. These people were 13 Arab tribes that lived in Yemen. Their settlements were located in Al-Ahqaf—an area between Oman and Hadramout. Prophet Hūd ﷺ came from the most famous and honorable family among them. He was the best of the 'Ād and was never a pagan. Like all Prophets, he was a believer; that is, a Muslim, and called his people to Islam.

The People of Prophet Hūd

Allāh has given the people of 'Ād many blessings and riches in this life. The 'Ādites were very strong and very tall. The tallest among them was 100 cubits while the shortest was 60 cubits. They lived on a fertile land, where there was a lot of water and were successful in agriculture and gardening. They also built grande palaces. Despite all these bounties, they were not grateful to their Creator. The 'Ādites were pagans and worshiped idols. They also oppressed other peoples, arrogantly considering themselves better than them. Allāh sent Prophet Hūd to call the people of 'Ād to Islam.

Hūd began to call on the 'Ādites to stop worshiping idols that do not create neither benefit nor harm, but to worship the One and Only Creator—Allāh. He also ordered them to stop sinning and oppressing people. However, only few followed his call and embraced Islam. They hid their faith fearing violence from the blasphemers. Most of the 'Ādites, out of arrogance, rejected the truth. They declared that they would not leave the religion of their fathers, and they called Prophet Hūd a fool and a crazy person. Moreover,

the ʿĀdites said that they could not believe that the messenger of Allāh is a person who eats and drinks like them. Prophet Hūd reminded them of the people of Prophet Nūh and the punishment that befell them because of their blasphemy; but the ʿĀdites still refused to accept Islam.

Punishment and death of the people of ʿĀd

Despite all the warnings of Prophet Hūd ﷺ, his people stubbornly denied the truth. They remained arrogant and stubborn and, mocking him, said, "Where is the punishment you speak of?! Show it to us if you are truthful!" Then Prophet Hūd ﷺ said to them, "Wait for the punishment from Allāh, which will certainly happen to you, and you cannot avoid it!" Allāh sent them a long drought, so they suffered greatly from thirst. Each time their suffering increased, Prophet Hūd reminded them that they would not be saved from this punishment if they did not become Muslims. They did not. Then, the drought became quite unbearable. Exhausted by thirst and hunger, the ʿĀdites began to ask their

idols for rain. They even sent a group of people to Mecca, hoping that their request would be answered there and began to wait for relief.

One day the 'Ādites saw clouds that appeared from the side of the valley that began to approach them. They became happy, thinking that these clouds would bring them the long-awaited rain. However, their joy was not to be; instead of relief, their death came with a strong and cold wind! When the non-believers saw the raging hurricane instead of the desired rain, their hearts became filled with fear and horror. Hoping to survive, they rushed to their homes, thinking that they would be safe there. Alas, their hope was in vain! A strong whirlwind lifted them into the air and destroyed them! A terrible tornado raged for eight days and seven nights. It lifted them into the air and threw them upside down on the ground, so that their heads tore off their bodies. Their headless dead long bodies lay on the ground like fallen trunks of palm trees. All of them died.

Nowadays, the area where the people of 'Ād lived is a desolate barren area where there are no plants, and no people or animals live.

Prophet Hūd ﷺ and his followers, by the Will of Allāh, were saved. After the death of the people of 'Ād, Prophet Hūd ﷺ went to Mecca and performed the Hajj. Prophet Hūd ﷺ lived for 150 years.

Prophet Hūd

PROPHET SALIH ﷺ

The People of Thamud

The people of Thamud resided in the western part of the Arabian Peninsula. They were blessed abundantly by Allāh, much like the people of 'Ād. They had fertile lands, plentiful vegetation, and abundant water springs. Despite these blessings, they took everything for granted and failed to show gratitude to their Creator who gave them all these bounties. Instead, they worshipped idols, indulged in worldly pleasures, and became obsessed with their wealth.

Prophet Sālih ﷺ, like Prophet Hud, was an Arab and was chosen to be the messenger for the people of Thamud. The tribe was named after one of Sālih's ancestors, Thamud, who was the great-grandson of Sam, the son of Prophet Nūh.

Coming from a noble family, Prophet Sālih was the wisest among the people of Thamud. He earnestly explained to them that idols could neither bring benefit nor harm since they held no power to create or control anything.

Prophet Sālih didn't seek power or reward from his people. His only desire was to guide them away from idol worship and lead them towards the right path of the true religion, seeking rewards from Allāh.

Witnessing Prophet Salih's determination and patience, the non-believers realized he wouldn't cease calling them to Islam. This concerned the leaders of the Thamud tribe, fearing that if their people followed Salih, their influence and authority would diminish. To test Prophet Salih, they demanded a miracle from him, believing that he would fail, and that would help their standing in the eyes of the people. They pointed to a specific rock and challenged him, saying, "Bring forth a camel from this rock," and they even described the appearance of the camel they expected to see.

The camel of Prophet Salih ﷺ

Upon the prayers of Prophet Salih ﷺ, Allāh granted him this miracle. A large camel with its baby emerged from a rock, right before the eyes of the people. Some were convinced and followed Prophet Salih, but many others remained arrogant and disbelieving.

Prophet Salih explained to his people that this camel was a special sign of his truthfulness, and he warned them not to harm or kill her, as doing so would lead to punishment. The camel would graze during the day, then return to the city in the evening, where she would talk to the people in pure Arabic, offering them milk. The people would place containers under her udder, and the containers would be filled with milk. The days passed with the camel grazing during the day and going to the mosque for the night.

The camel and the people of Thamud had a unique arrangement. They shared the same well for drinking water, taking turns, and on the days the camel drank, she provided them with milk to drink. However, some wicked individuals in  Thamud saw the camel as a threat to their power, as more people were inclined to follow Prophet Sālih because of her presence. They devised a plot to kill the camel, despite Prophet Sālih's repeated warnings about the consequences of disobeying Allāh's commands.

Nine individuals carried out the brutal killing of the camel, led by a man named Qudar, the worst and ugliest among them with a pug nose. One threw an arrow on her so Qudar rushed and killed her with his sword. The camel fell on the ground dead with a pool of blood. The baby camel escaped to a nearby mountain, entered a rock, and disappeared there. It was a Wednesday.

Punishment of the Thamudians

Allāh revealed to Prophet Sālih that the non-believers would not accept Islam, and they would face punishment after three days. The Thamudians decided to act against Prophet Sālih and his family before the three days were up. However, Allāh protected Sālih, and as they approached the mosque to kill him, stones from the sky fell upon them, destroying the criminals.

The three-day punishment began on Thursday. The non-believers' faces turned yellow, and their bodies were covered with horrible ulcers. On Friday, their faces turned red like blood, and on Saturday, their faces turned black like tar. The believers with Prophet Sālih left the city on Saturday night.

On Sunday, the blisters on the non-believers' skin began to open. Angel Gabriel appeared and emitted a deafening cry, causing their hearts to rupture in their chests, leading to immediate death. The intensity of the sound and horror was too much for them to bear. Their strong houses were also shaken and destroyed, burying them beneath the ruins. Their city was between Madinah and Tabuk, it is known today as Mada'in Sālih, or Al-Hijr.

Upon witnessing the destruction, Prophet Sālih and the believers left the land of Thamud. He then journeyed to the Land of Sham, eventually settling in Palestine and later moving to Mecca, where he lived a life of worship until he passed away at the age of 58.

PROPHET AL-KHADIR

Do you know who the longest living human being is? Have you heard of the "Spring of Life"? it is time for the fascinating story of Al-Khadir!

His name was Balya'. He became known as Al-Khadir, which is derived from the Arabic word "Akhdar" meaning green, because he once sat on a barren piece of land that turned green at his touch.

The story of Al-Khadir

Al-Khadir is known to have the longest life among the sons of Adam. He is the cousin of Prophet Abraham's grandfather, Allāh willed for Al-Khadir to have an exceptionally long life, and he is still alive to this day. He was once part of the army of Dhul-Qarnayn, a pious ruler who ruled the earth from east to west. Dhul-Qarnayn expressed his desire for a longer life to do more good deeds, and upon hearing this, Angel Rafaeel informed Dhul-Qarnayn about the

"Spring of Life." Drinking from this spring would grant one an extended life until Allāh willed their death. Al-Khadir asked Rafaeel if he knows the place of this spring. Rafaeel answered, "No, but we, the angels, talk

with each other in the sky and mention that Allāh created a dark place on earth that no human or genie has ever reached. We think the spring is in that dark place."

Dhul-Qarnayn, prepared an army with Al-Khadir holding its banner and embarked on a journey to find the "Spring of Life." After twelve years of travel, they reached a dark place caused by heavy fog-like smoke. At one point, Al-Khadir separated from the group and went down alone into a valley. There, he found the spring, its water whiter than milk and sweeter than honey. He drank from it, made wudu' (ablution), and bathed.

Al-Khadir's life took a different path afterward. He became isolated on the surface of the sea, hidden from people's sight. Despite his isolation, he occasionally appears to good people, sharing his knowledge and wisdom. Prophet Moses also encountered Al-Khadir, as mentioned in the Qur'an (Surat Al-Kahf). Al-Khadir will eventually pass away before the Day of Judgment.

Al-Khadr is considered by some scholars to be a pious person (waliyy), not a prophet.

PROPHET IBRAHIM ﷺ

Prophet Ibrahim (Abraham) is one of the best prophets, second only to Prophet Muhammad ﷺ.

He was born in Babylon in Iraq. At that time, Babylon was a center of a big kingdom and had lot of riches. There were many beautiful palaces. Many people lived in luxury, but they were ignorant and misguided. They worshiped idols that they made with their hands, the sun, the moon and the stars. They had a powerful king called Numrud. He was a tyrant and a blasphemer. Seeing the ignorance of his people, Numrud said about himself that he is god and ordered the people to worship him.

The Birth of Ibrahim ﷺ

One day, the stargazers, who claimed to predict the future by observing the stars and communicating with devils who eavesdrop on the angels in the sky, brought troubling news to King Numrud. They informed him that a boy named Ibrahim was destined to be born in the kingdom of Babylon, and he would not follow the king's religion and would destroy the idols worshipped in the land. So Numrud ordered all pregnant women in the kingdom to be imprisoned and placed under his watchful eye. When any of them delivered a boy, Numrud would order that this newborn be killed. Only Ibrahim's mother escaped this terrible fate—she was very young, and her pregnancy went unnoticed. When it was time to give birth, Ibrahim's mother went to a cave near her house and gave birth to a child there. She took care of her newborn, closed the entrance of the cave, and returned home. She used to visit him regularly and noticed that he was growing very quickly—in a day he grew up as ordinary children grew up in a month. Ibrahim stayed in the cave for fifteen months. Years passed and Ibrahim became a young man.

Prophethood of Ibrahim

Like all the prophets, Ibrahim was a believer and worshipped Allāh. He never worshipped other than Allāh, not even for a second. He never worshipped idols, the stars, the sun, or the moon. When he became a prophet, he began to call his people to leave worshiping idols and other creations. First, Ibrahim called his own father, Azar, to Islam. Azar was a non-believer, who not only worshipped idols but also made and sold them to others. He urged his father to abandon worshiping idols that do not create anything and do not deserve to be worshipped and to worship only Allāh, but Azar was arrogant and did not follow his son's advice. He even threatened Ibrahim saying that he would kill him. However, this did not weaken Ibrahim; he firmly continued to preach the truth to the people.

Ibrahim ﷺ Destroys the Idols

On the day of the pagan festival, while everyone left the city to celebrate in orchards and gardens, Prophet Ibrahim stayed behind. He entered the house where the idols were kept, finding many small ones and one large idol, which was highly revered by the people. With an axe in hand, he destroyed all the small idols and then hung the axe around the neck of the big idol, demonstrating the weakness of these lifeless statues. Prophet Ibrahim ﷺ wanted to show the people that these idols were powerless and did not deserve worship, hoping that they would abandon idolatry and embrace Islam.

After the celebration, when the people returned to the city and saw the destruction of their idols, they became furious and sought to find the culprit. Suspecting that Prophet Ibrahim ﷺ was responsible, they decided to hold a trial for him.

Standing in front of the enraged crowd, he firmly replied that the biggest idol was to blame for what happened, and added: "Ask them yourself if they speak!" He spoke in such a way as to force the non-believers to admit that idols cannot even speak and were unable to defend themselves. In this way, non-believers could clearly understand that the idols they worshipped have no life and do not create benefit or harm. Prophets never lie, Prophet Ibrahim ﷺ was not lying when he said that the greatest idol was to blame for what happened. His words meant that the big idol caused the destruction of the rest. For the non-believers exalted it the most, and this caused Ibrahim to be very angry for the sake of Allah and pushed him to destroy the idols. Despite the correctness of Ibrahim's argument, the people did not accept the truth out of their stubbornness and decided to punish Ibrahim.

The Debate between Prophet Ibrahim ﷺ and the Tyrant King

After Ibrahim gave clear proof to his people of the falsehood of their religion, they rejected his call and brought him to their tyrant king, Numrud, who claimed to be god. Numrud asked arrogantly: "And whom do you worship and call others to worship?!" "My Lord, the One who gives life and death," replied Ibrahim, ﷺ. Numrud falsely answered: "I give life and death. Let them bring to me two persons condemned to the death penalty, one I will order to be executed, and the other I will pardon!" Immediately Ibrahim said: "Verily, Allāh commands the sun to rise from the east. Make it rise from the west?!" The astonished Numrud did not find any answer. Prophet Ibrahim showed that the humiliated Numrud is not god and that there is no god except Allāh!

The Miracle of the Resurrection of the Birds

Numrud wanted to take revenge on Prophet Ibrahim for the shame he experienced and said to him: "Ask your Lord to revive the dead, otherwise I will kill you." Prophet Ibrahim ﷺ, was not afraid of Numrud's threats. He made a prayer and asked Allāh to revive the dead. Ibrahim hoped that, seeing this miracle, perhaps Numrud would believe. Allāh answered Ibrahim's supplication and ordered Ibrahim to take four birds: a green peacock, a red rooster, a black crow and a white dove, and after slaughtering them to cut their dead bodies into small parts. Prophet Ibrahim mixed all these parts and left the bird's bodies on the tops of seven mountains but took their heads with him. Prophet Ibrahim ﷺ stood in a place where he could see all these mountain's peaks, and, holding the heads of the birds in his hands, he said: "By the Will of Allāh, I call you. Come to me." At that moment, the parts of each bird began to come together: feathers began to unite with feathers, flesh with flesh, and their bodies took on their original appearance. Souls returned to them, and the birds rushed to their heads, which Ibrahim held in his hands. Whenever Prophet Ibrahim ﷺ offered the head to its proper body, it would connect with it and the bird returned to how it was exactly before it

died. Even after such an amazing miracle, the people of Babylon and their king Numrud did not believe in Allāh, the Almighty.

The Big Fire and the Big Miracle

The hatred of the non-believers towards Prophet Ibrahim grew stronger, and they were determined to kill him. They dug a huge hole and began to carry firewood into it from everywhere. Even sick women vowed to collect firewood for this if they recovered. After a huge amount of firewood was collected, they started a fire. A bright flame broke out and began to flare up with a very strong force. The fire was so strong that the sparks that rose high into the sky burned the birds flying above it! Even the people themselves could not come close to this fire to throw Ibrahim there! The cursed Iblees (Satan) appeared in the form of a man and taught them how to build a catapult to throw Ibrahim in the fire from a distance. The pagans built the catapult, seized Prophet Ibrahim ﷺ, tied his hands, and put him on the bowl of the catapult. At this moment, Ibrahim supplicated Allāh and said: "There is no God but You! You are clear from any imperfection! Praise be to You! Everything is in Your Power. You have no partners." Ibrahim relied completely on his Lord. The catapult was activated. People watched this spectacle from afar and believed that Ibrahim was burned. However, Allāh granted Prophet Ibrahim ﷺ, a great miracle: the fire did not burn him and did not cause him any harm. Even his clothes were intact. Only the ropes with which he was bound were burned without damaging his skin. After several days, the fire started to weaken. Numrud had no doubt that Ibrahim burned and died. Standing on top of a tower and carefully peering into the fire, he saw that Ibrahim was alive! Ibrahim ﷺ was sitting inside the fire next to a man who looked like him. The tyrant turned to his subjects: "It seemed to me that I saw Ibrahim alive! Build me a higher tower so that I can better see what is going on there." Numrud climbed the tower and saw that Ibrahim was really alive. He called out to Ibrahim, "Can you come out?" Prophet Ibrahim ﷺ replied: "Yes." When Prophet came out of the fire unharmed, he was asked who was sitting next to him. He replied that it was the angel of the shadow, giving him company.

Emigration of Prophet Ibrahim ﷺ to Sham

Despite this great miracle, Numrud and his people remained unbelievers. Few people followed the call of Prophet Ibrahim ﷺ, but hid their Islam from others so Numrud would not harm them. Then, Allāh ordered Ibrahim to move to the land of Sham, the blessed land where many prophets lived at different times. Prophet Ibrahim, along with his wife Sarah left Babylon, and went to Sham with his nephew Lut.

The Demise of Numrud

Despite the irrefutable evidence and the great miracles that the stubborn Numrud witnessed, he did not accept Islam. Numrud was afflicted with a mosquito who entered his head through one of his nostrils and who lived there for 400 years, torturing him. During all this time, he suffered unbearable pain, which was calmed only when Numrud hit himself in the head. He also ordered others to do the same; so he was beaten on the head with hands and shoes, and this continued until his death.

The call of the people of Harran

On the way to Sham (the Land of the Levant), Prophet Ibrahim ﷺ and his companions passed through the area of Harran, the inhabitants of which, worshiped seven bodies in the sky-the sun, the moon and five stars. Prophet Ibrahim ﷺ told them that neither the stars nor the sun nor the moon are worthy of worship. He gave them evidence, explaining to the people that these bodies change; they appear and then disappear. They change their location and anything that changes cannot be god, because it itself needs someone who changes it-the Creator, the Eternal, the One without a beginning and without an end, the One who does not change, does not disappear and does not die. The people of Harran, like the people of Babylon, rejected the call of Prophet Ibrahim ﷺ. Ibrahim ﷺ and his companions continued their journey to Sham.

Travel to Egypt

Prophet Ibrahim ﷺ reached Palestine, the center of the Land of Sham, and lived there for some time until a severe drought set in. He and his wife then left to Egypt. At that time, an evil non-believer pharoah ruled Egypt. He had a disgusting habit: when a beautiful married woman appeared in his kingdom, he ordered her to be brought to him and took possession of her by force. Sarah was a pious Muslimah and among the most beautiful women. When Prophet Ibrahim and Sarah entered the land of Egypt, the assistants of the pharaoh immediately reported to him that they saw a woman of extraordinary beauty who arrived in his land. The pharaoh ordered Ibrahim to be brought in and asked him: "Who is this woman with you?" Ibrahim guessed the bad intentions of Pharaoh and realized that if he said that this was his wife, Pharaoh would kill him and take Sarah for himself. Allāh bestowed on Prophet Ibrahim ﷺ special wisdom and foresight, so Ibrahim replied: "She is my sister," meaning "sister in faith, in Islam," and it was true. The pharoah ordered her to come to the palace. Prophet Ibrahim ﷺ returned to his wife and told her of his meeting with the pharaoh. He said, "O Sarah! Apart from us, there is no longer a pair of believers on earth—husband and wife. When he asked me about you, I replied that you were my sister (meaning in Islam)." Sarah performed ablution and prayed to Allāh that He would protect her from the evil of this pharoah. She then went to his palace. When the pharoah saw Sarah, he was struck by her beauty. He stretched out his hand, wanting to touch her, but at this moment, by Allāh's Will, his hand froze, as if paralyzed. He could not move it and asked Sarah to make supplication to Allāh so that his hand would be cured, and promised that he would not touch her again. Sarah complied with this request, and the hand of the pharaoh returned to normal. However, this bad man did not give up his intention and again extended his hand to her. Again, he could not touch her—his hand was paralyzed even more so than the first time. Then the pharoah again began to ask Sarah to make a dua' for him and promised not to harm her. Sarah did, and by the Will of Allāh, the tyrant's hand became healthy again. Frightened and surprised, the tyrant called the assistant who brought Sarah and said to him: "Get her out of here! You brought me a genie, not a human! Get her out of my land! Give her the slave woman Hajar as a gift and let her go!" Then Sarah and Hajar returned to Prophet Ibrahim ﷺ. They found him praying. After leaving Egypt, Prophet Ibrahim ﷺ, together with Sarah, returned to Sham.

Birth of Isma'il

Years passed, and Sarah and Ibrahim had no children. Sarah was barren, this means she was unable to have children. She was saddened that her husband had no children. At that time, Ibrahim was eighty-six years old, and Sarah was over seventy years old. Then Sarah gave Ibrahim her slave Hajar in the hope that she would give birth to a child for him. Soon, Hajar gave birth to a boy, Isma'il, who also became a prophet.

The appearance of Zamzam Water

After some time, Prophet Ibrahim ﷺ took Hajar with Isma'il, who was still an infant, to Mecca. At that time, Mecca was a deserted area where there was no water, no people, and no buildings. The Kaabah was not even there; it was destroyed during the Flood that happened at the time of Prophet Nuh ﷺ. Only its foundation remained. Prophet Ibrahim ﷺ left Hajar with her baby near a large tree. He left with them a leather bag filled with water and some dates. When Hajar saw that Ibrahim was leaving, she followed him and asked: "O Ibrahim! Are you going to leave us here, in this deserted place?!" She repeated this question without getting an answer. She then asked: "Did Allāh order you to do that?" He replied: "Yes!" Then, with strong reliance on Allāh, she said, "In that case, we will not be lost!" Prophet Ibrahim ﷺ worried about his family, leaving them alone in a deserted place, but firmly relied on the mercy of Allāh. When he was a bit away from them, he turned towards the Kaabah and made a du'a to Allāh: "O Lord! I have settled some of my offspring in a barren valley by Your Sacred House so they would perform the prayer. O Lord, make the hearts of some people yearn towards them and provide them with fruits for which they would give thanks." Hajar breastfed Isma'il while she drank from the water and ate from the dates Ibrahim left them. Then the water ran out, and after a while, she became thirsty. Isma'il began to cry from hunger. Unable to look any longer at the suffering of her baby, she went to look for water. Hajar climbed the nearest hill As-Safa. She looked down to the valley, hoping to see people or water, but saw nothing. Then she went down and quickly went to another hill, Al-Marwah. She climbed to the very top, but even there she did not find water. So she walked, rushing from As-Safa to Al-Marwah seven times. When Hajar was at the top of the Marwah hill, she heard a sound. She shouted: "Help us, if you can!" And then she saw Angel Jibreel. Jibreel struck the ground with his foot, and a source of pure and fresh water gushed out from under the ground. This source appeared not far from the tree, under which little Isma'il lay. Hajar fenced this water from all sides so that it would not spread over the ground and so she could collect it. Jibreel said to her: "Do not fear! Allāh will save you. Soon at this place,—he pointed to the hill,—there will be a Sacred House (the Kaabah), where people will come from everywhere to worship Allāh. This mosque will be built by this boy together with his father." The water, which by the Will of Allah appeared in the valley of Mecca and saved Hajar and baby Isma'il, still exists nowadays. It is known as Zamzam.

Arrival of the Jurhum tribe to Mecca

Not far from the place where Hajar settled with her son, the Arab tribe of Jurhum passed by. Seeing birds circling the area from a distance, they realized that there must be water there. They went and asked Lady Hajar for permission to settle down in this place. She agreed, and they set up their tents near the blessed spring. Hajar was glad that, now, she and Isma'il were no longer alone in this valley. Since that time, the area of Mecca has gradually turned into a city where lot of people lived. Isma'il grew up among the Arabs of Jurhum tribe and learned Arabic perfectly. The Arabs loved him for his beauty, knoweldge, and excellent qualities. When Isma'il grew up, he got married to a woman from jurhum. Thus the dua' of Prophet Ibrahim ﷺ, which he said when he left Hajar and Isma'il was answered. Allāh protected them. Water appeared and people who love and respected them came and lived among them. Ibrahim, who was living in Palestine far from Mecca, used to visit Hajar and

Isma'il on the Burak, a riding animal from Paradise. Prophet Ibrahim ﷺ used to set out from Sham to Mecca early in the morning, and by the afternoon he was already back to Palestine.

The story of Prophet Ibrahim's Sacrifice ﷺ

When Isma'il grew up, Prophet Ibrahim ﷺ had a dream—as if he was sacrificing his beloved son! When he woke up, he realized that this dream was the command of Allah, because the dreams of the Prophets are true! This was another test of Prophet Ibrahim ﷺ in his obedience to his Creator! After all, what could be more difficult for a father than to sacrifice a long-awaited and beloved child with his own hands! The heart of Prophet Ibrahim ﷺ was heavy, but he did not hesitate for a second in his intention to fulfill the order of Allāh! He said to Isma'il, "Come with me to offer a sacrifice for Allāh." Prophet Ibrahim ﷺ took a knife and a rope and they went together. When they reached the mountains, Isma'il asked his father: "Where is your Qurban (the sacrifice)?" Prophet Ibrahim ﷺ answered him: "Son, I saw in a dream that I was sacrificing you! What do you say to that?" Isma'il did not resist or became angry, but said: "Father! Do what Allāh commanded you, and I will be patient by the Will of Allāh!" With this, Isma'il showed an excellent example of patience and support to his father in obeying God. Isma'il understood that it was not easy for his father to lose his own son. Wanting to ease this matter on him, he said, "Tie me tight so I don't move. Try not to let my blood get on your clothes otherwise, my mother will notice and grieve. Let the knife pass quickly down my throat to make it easier for me to die. And when you see my mother, then give her my salam." Prophet Ibrahim ﷺ, touched by the courage and nobility of Isma'il, wept, embraced and kissed his son. He said to him: "You are a great help to me in obeying Allāh!" Then Prophet Ibrahim ﷺ put his son on his side, but when he tried to cut his throat, the knife did not cut, instead it turned to the blunt side! No matter how hard Ibrahim tried—the knife did not cut! Then Prophet Ibrahim ﷺ heard a voice saying, "O Ibrahim! You have done what you had been told!" It was Jibreel who brought for sacrifice a large beautiful ram from Paradise with white wool and large horns, which had grazed in Paradise for forty years. Thus, by His mercy, Allāh gave Ibrahim relief, and Isma'il survived! It was a great trial that showed Ibrahim's strong faith!

Construction of the Holy Kaabah

During the Flood, the structure of the Kaabah was destroyed—only its foundation remained. When Prophet Ibrahim ﷺ received a command from Allāh to rebuild the Kaabah, he went to Mecca. There, he said to his son Isma'il, "Allāh has commanded you to help me in bulding the Sacred House." Jibreel showed Prophet Ibrahim

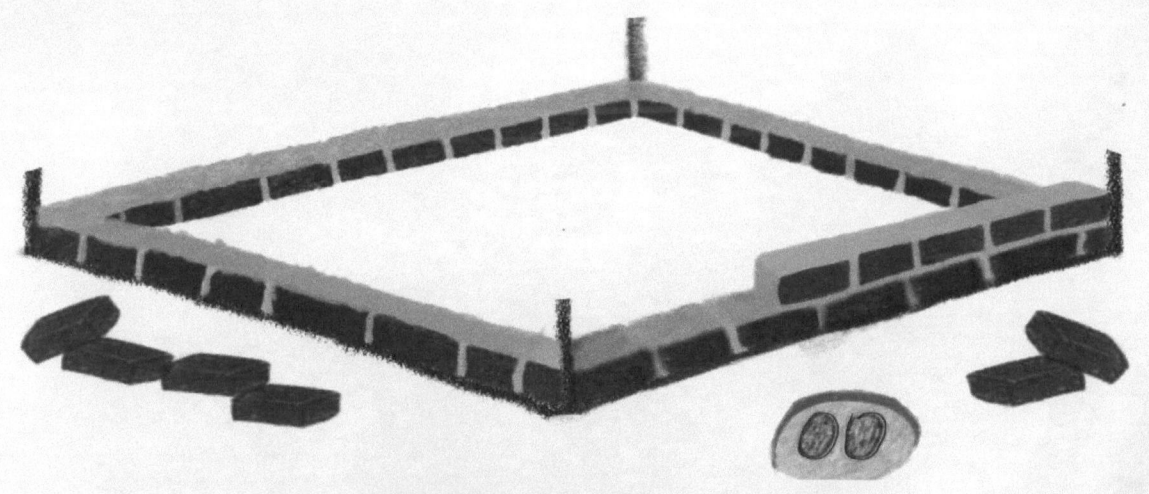

the place where the foundation of the Kaabah was located, then Ibrahim and Isma'il began to build it—Isma'il gave the stones to his father, and Ibrahim laid them row by row. Prophet Ibrahim ﷺ stood on a special stone from Paradise—when he finished laying one row, this stone rose so that the next row could be laid until they completed the construction of the Kaabah. The stone on which Prophet Ibrahim ﷺ stood has survived to this day. It is known as "Maqam Ibrahim"—"the place of standing of Ibrahim". It bears the footprints of this great prophet. When the Kaabah was built, Ibrahim ﷺ asked Isma'il to bring a beautiful stone, which he would set in

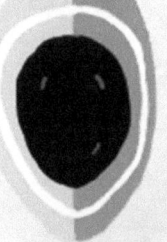

the corner of the building, and it would be a sign for people. Angel Jibreel appeared with a stone—a ruby from Paradise—which became known later as the "Black Stone", because it turned black due to the pagans touching it. Ibrahim put this stone in its place.

After the Holy Kaabah was restored, Jibreel taught Ibrahim ﷺ how to perform the Hajj rituals (Pilgrimage). Then, Ibrahim ﷺ and Isma'il performed Hajj. Later, Isma'il became a prophet too.

The News of Isḥāq

Ibrahim kept visiting from time to time Hajar and his son Isma'il in Mecca, while he and Sarah lived in Palestine. As we said Sarah was barren. She was a very good woman too. When she was 90 years old, something amazing happened to her and her husband. How did such good news come to them? One day, guests, strangers to Ibrahim, came. They entered his house and greeted Ibrahim ﷺ. He returned their greeting. He thought they are travelers and asked his wife to help prepare a meal for them. Prophet Ibrahim ﷺ was very generous and liked to be good to his guests. Ibrahim ﷺ offered them meat from the best calf he had, but when they were served the food, it became noticeable that they were not interested in it. This alerted Ibrahim ﷺ, and he asked: "Why don't you eat?" Then the guests said, "Don't be surprised. We are angels." They informed him too that they are on their way to the cities of the sinful people that did not listen to Prophet Lut ﷺ, to punish them. Thus, Prophet Ibrahim ﷺ understood why they did not even touch the feast! After all, angels do not sleep, do not drink and do not eat. Then the angels gave Ibrahim and Sarah the good news about the birth of a son for them. They were shocked by this news! Sarah said in surprise: "But I am a barren old woman! How can I give birth?!" The angels told her: "This is the Will of Allāh." Prophet Ibrahim ﷺ was also joyfully surprised. The angels who came to visit Prophet Ibrahim in human form were Jibreel, the best angel and the other two honorable angels, Mikail and Israfeel. They informed Prophet Ibrahim ﷺ that his son would be wise, pious and would be a prophet. This son was named Isḥāq (Isaac).

The High Status of Prophet Ibrahim

Abraham is one of the five best prophets called ulul-'azm in Arabic: Muhammad, Abraham, Moses, Jesus and Nuh. Ten Holy Scrolls (suhuf) were revealed to Prophet Abraham ﷺ. In each of the five daily prayers, we mention Prophet Abraham ﷺ by reciting As-Salat Al-Ibrahimiyyah. The Kaabah, the Black Stone, Maqam Ibrahim, Hajj rituals and 'Eid Al-Adha remind us of the life of Prophet Abraham ﷺ. All the Prophets after Abraham mentioned in the Holy Qur'an were his descendants. Prophet Muhammad ﷺ, the last and best prophet is one of the offsprings of Prophet Isma'il, the eldest son of Abraham. There were many prophets from Isaac's lineage, and the last of them was Prophet Jesus ﷺ. Therefore, Prophet Ibrahim ﷺ was called "Abul-Anbiya'", which means the father of the prophets. The lineage of the Prophet Abraham ﷺ is the only one in humanity that had prophets in four generations in a row: Joseph (son), Jacob (father), Isaac (grandfather), and Abraham (great grandfather).

Abraham ﷺ lived for 200 years. Sarah died before Abraham, and he buried her in a cave near the city of Hebron (Al-Khalil). When Prophet Abraham ﷺ died, his sons Isma'il and Isaac buried him in the same cave, near Lady Sarah.

PROPHET ISMA'IL

Isma'il was a prophet sent to the Arab tribes in the area where he lived, the tribe of Al-'Amaleek, and the inhabitants of Yemen to call them for Islam.

Isma'il supported Prophet Ibrahim. He was a loving son, listened to his advice, and helped his father in his affairs. After Prophet Isma'il got married, Ibrahim continued to visit his son from time to time. Then Ibrahim was absent for some time before he returned to Mecca. He saw Isma'il at work under a tree at the well of Zamzam sharpening arrows. Isma'il saw his father, whom he missed very much, and approached him.

Ibrahim informed Isma il that Allah ordered him to build a sacred house—the Kaabah, and pointed to Isma'il its place. Together they built the Honorable Kaabah. Isma'il brought stones, and Ibrahim laid them.

Prophet Isma'il had twelve sons from his second wife, and from his lineage came the Arabs of the Hijaz.

Among the descendants of Isma'il, only one prophet emerged—the final and greatest of all prophets—Prophet Muhammad.

He lived for 137 years and was buried alongside his mother Hajar in a place called "Hijr Isma'il" in Mecca.

PROPHET ISHAQ

Ishāq, the second son of Ibrahim from Lady Sarah, was sent to the people of Canaan in Palestine where he lived. He called people to Islam and to worship Allāh.

Prophet Ibrahim advised Ishaq to marry a girl from their family. Ishāq married Rafqah (Rebekah).

Initially, they had no children, but after supplicating to Allāh, they were blessed with twin boys named Al-'Is (Esau) and Ya'qub (Jacob), who later became a prophet too.

Many prophets were descended from Prophet Ishāq, including 'Isa, who was sent before Prophet Muhammad.

Ishāq lived for 180 years and was buried by his sons in the cave next to his father and mother in Hebron, Palestine.

PROPHET LUT ﷺ

Prophet Lut ﷺ was the nephew of Prophet Ibrahim ﷺ. Like his uncle, Lut was not an Arab, and his name is not Arabic nor derived from an Arabic word.

Like all the prophets, he believed in Allah and followed the right path, never committing blasphemy.

He was born in Babylon. He was the first to believe in Prophet Ibrahim ﷺ and went with him when he moved to the land of the Levant (Sham). He also accompanied him on his other trips. Then Allāh gave him the Revelation and sent him to the people of Sodom.

People of Prophet Lut ﷺ

The city of Sodom was near the Dead Sea in modern eastern Jordan. Four smaller cities were located near Sodom.

The people of Sodom were one of the most sinful nations. They sinned openly, without any shame. When men gathered for entertainment, they committed an ugly sin together. They were the first to commit the sin of sodomy. They also attacked and robbed travelers passing by.

Prophet Lut ﷺ called these people to Islam and also forbade them to commit sins. But despite the efforts of Prophet Lut ﷺ, they did not accept the faith and continued to sin even more.

They called Lut a liar and did not believe in the punishment he had warned them with, and even threatened to expel him from the city. Then Lut ﷺ asked Allāh to grant him victory over these non-believers. Allah the Almighty sent three honorable angels to punish them—Gabriel, Mikael and Israfil.

Guests of the Prophet Lut ﷺ

The three angels, in the form of beautiful young men, went to the city of Sodom after they visited Prophet Ibrahim ﷺ in Palestine. While there, they told Ibrahim they were going to Sodom to punish its inhabitants for their blasphemy and ugly sins. Hearing this, Prophet Ibrahim ﷺ became worried about his nephew Lut who lives in Sodom, but the angels reassured him, saying that Allāh would save Prophet Lut, his followers, and his relatives except for his non-believer wife.

At noon, the angels came to the city of Sodom and went to the house of Lut ﷺ. At first, Prophet Lut thought they are travelers. He greeted and invited them into his house. He became worried that his people would know about them and try to commit sodomy with them.

Soon, what Prophet Lut ﷺ feared happened. His non-believer wife told her people about her husband guests—unusually handsome young men, the likes of whom she had never seen before. As soon as this news spread in the city, the inhabitants of Sodom rushed to the house of Lut intending to do evil acts. Prophet Lut ﷺ urged them to abandon their dirty intentions. He spoke to them gently, with wisdom, hoping that they would listen to him. He urged them to do what is lawful in the Shariʿah, and to marry the girls living in this city, and not to desire sin with men.

Prophet Lut ﷺ locked the door of his house to protect his guests. Nevertheless, they tried to break down the door to get inside. Seeing what Prophet Lut ﷺ is going through, the angels told him that they are not humans, rather they are angels sent by Allāh to destroy this city. The angels instructed Lut to leave the city with his family at night before the punishment would befall the non-believers at dawn. They also told him when he leaves not to turn back and look, so as not to see the terrible punishment.

When Prophet Lut ﷺ locked the door of the house to keep the non-believers out, they kept trying to open the door and go inside. Gabriel asked Allāh for permission to punish the wicked so Gabriel went out and hit the non-believers in the face with the edge of his wing. As a result, they became blind. Their eyes have completely disappeared—as if they never existed! They then left, groping their way, threatening Prophet Lut ﷺ that they would still get to him.

Punishment of the inhabitants of Sodom

At dawn, a terrible punishment befell the inhabitants of Sodom. Angel Gabriel, with his immense strength, lifted the cities along with the people and animals high into the sky and then flipped them over, causing their destruction. A powerful cry from the sky and a hail of stones were also unleashed upon them, marking their demise. Each stone carried the name of the person it was meant for.

Angel Gabriel lifted up the cities of the unbelievers with one feather of his wings. Angels are super strong! Gabriel has 600 wings; each wing would fill the entire horizon when spread. Gabriel raised these cities, along with the people, 400,000 of them, and their animals so high that the angels in the first heaven heard the crowing of their roosters and the barking of their dogs.

Before the sun rose, the wicked people of Sodom met their end, while Prophet Lut ﷺ and his followers, who believed in Allāh, were spared from the punishment. As they were leaving the city, Prophet Lut's non-believer wife heard the roar of destruction, so she turned around and cried out, "Oh, my people!" At that moment, she was struck by a stone thus meeting her fate along with the rest of the wicked inhabitants.

The story of the punishment of Sodom reminds us of the consequences of sinful behavior and the importance of listening to the message of the prophets. It also tells us the importance of faith and belief in Allāh's guidance. Prophet Lut's unwavering devotion to Allāh and his righteous followers serve as an example of staying on the right path and calling others to righteousness.

PROPHET SHU'AYB

The Origin of the Prophet Shu'ayb

Prophet Shu'ayb was one of the four Arab Prophets: Hud, Salih, Shu'ayb, and Muhammad. He belonged to the people of Madyan (Midianites). Prophet Shu'ayb was known for his eloquence especially when he called people to Islam.

The call of Prophet Shu'ayb to Monotheism

When evil spread among the people, Allāh the Almighty bestowed the Revelation upon Shu'ayb and commanded him to call his people to Islam. He urged them to abandon the worship of creations and embrace monotheism, worshipping only Allāh. Additionally, Prophet Shu'ayb forbade them from committing sins and ordered them to weigh and measure fairly when they buy and sell. Prophet Shu'ayb's patience and perseverance were evident as he tried various ways to reach out to the people and call them to the straight path. He warned them of the severe punishment awaiting non-believers in the Hereafter and reminded them of the fate of previous non-believing nations, including those of Prophet Hud, Prophet Salih, and Prophet Lut.

Punishment of Madyan people

Despite all the warnings, only a few believed in Prophet Shu'ayb ﷺ while the majority mocked Shu'ayb, called him a liar, and threatened to kill him by throwing stones at him. They said to Shu'ayb, "Truly, you are bewitched and do not understand what you are saying! You are a human being just like us! We think you're a liar!" If you are truly a prophet, then ask Allāh to bring down punishment on us from heaven!" Seeing that they did not want to accept the truth, Prophet Shu'ayb ﷺ made dua'; he said: "O Lord! Show them who is on the right path! Truly, You are just, and You give victory!" Allāh answered Shu'ayb supplication and sent on them severe heat as punishment. For seven days there was not even a faint breath of wind. Neither water, nor shade, nor underground shelters helped them from this heat. In search of salvation, the Midianites left the city. They sought refuge under a big cloud. In the shadow of this cloud, they felt cool and began to call the others there. When everyone gathered under this cloud, fiery lightning struck them. The earth beneath them shook, and from heaven came the terrible cry of an angel because of which their voices silenced—all the non-believers died! Prophet Shu'ayb ﷺ and those who believed in his message, were saved. As he left the land, Shu'ayb ﷺ said, "O people! I have called you to the true path, and I have conveyed to you all that I have been ordered to. I gave you advice, but you didn't listen to it, so how can I grieve over a disbelieving people" Prophet Shu'ayb ﷺ lived for 242 years and was buried in nowadays Jordan.

Prophet Shu'ayb

EPILOGUE

We hope you enjoyed reading this book and learned precious lessons from the stories of the beloved prophets of Allah, may peace be upon them.

You reached the end of this book; continue reading more stories about the prophets and their noble mission in volume 2!

إن شاء الله تعالى

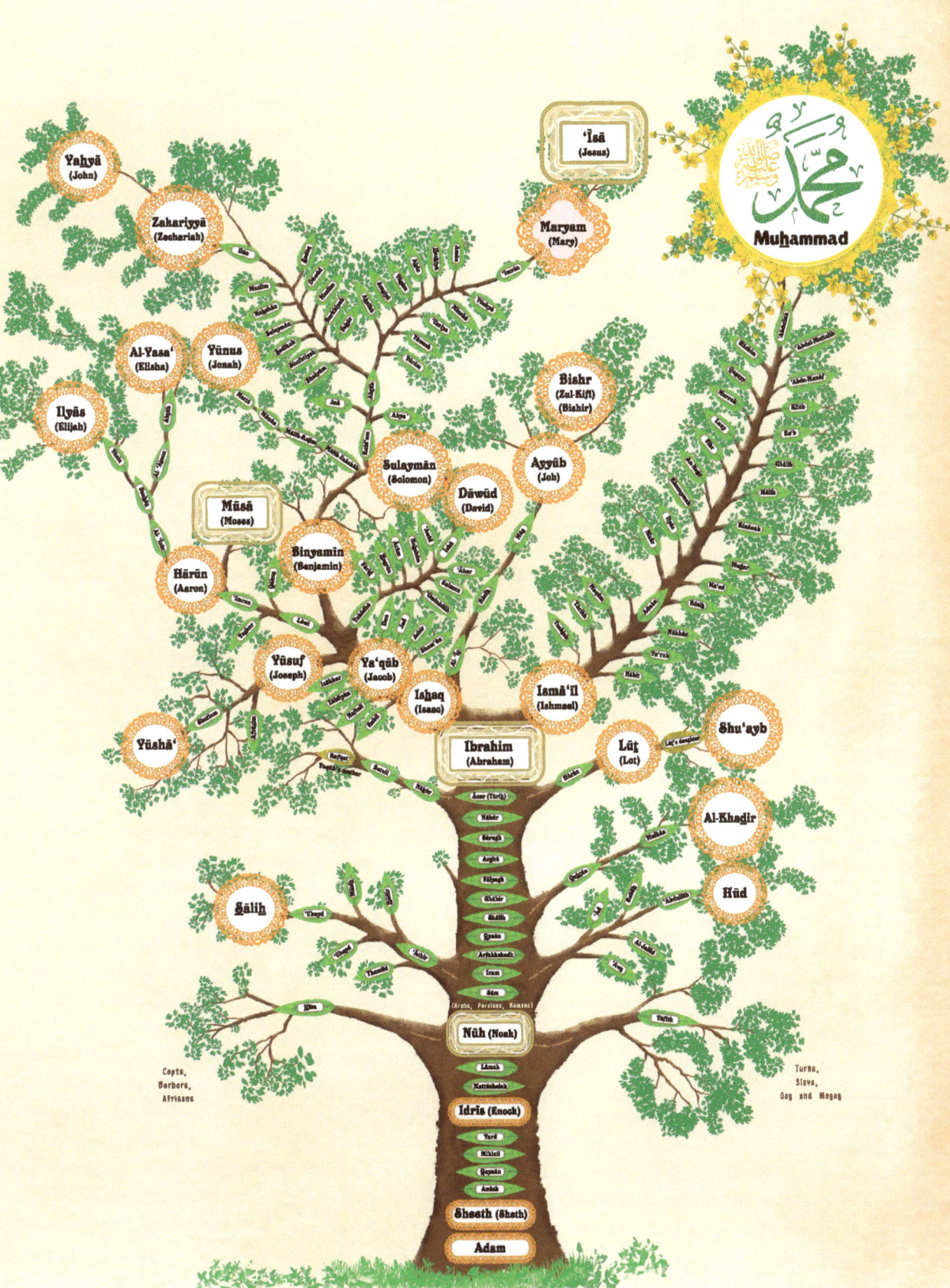

www.ingramcontent.com/pod-product-compliance
Lightning Source LLC
Chambersburg PA
CBHW042001150426
43194CB00002B/88